The nature of liberation is direct, simple and as natural as breathing. Many will come across it and shuffle quickly back to that which they think they can know and do. But there are those with whom the invitation will resonate... they will suddenly see and be ready to let go of all seeking, even for that which they have called enlightenment.

Introduction

Whilst we remain locked within the apparent experience of being separate individuals living in an existence with which we have to negotiate, we live in a state of dreaming.

In that dream state, all that we do is governed by the law of opposites in which every so-called positive act is exactly and equally balanced by its opposite.

Therefore all of our individual attempts to make our lives work, to reach perfection or to attain personal liberation, are neutralised.

We discover, through deep reflection and understanding, that as long as we continue in this dream we are, in reality, living in a circle. We are on a wheel on which everything is continually repeating itself over and over again in differing images. It is consciousness delighting in a creation that is both constrained and liberated. And despite what we believe about our individuality and free will, we come to see that we are only dreamed characters reacting and responding from a set of conditioned and historical belief systems.

All of classic religion, art and science in a world that we see as progressive, comes within the parameters of this perfectly balanced and exactly neutral state which serves only to reflect another possibility. In terms of

actual liberation nothing is happening. What we have apparently created is apparently destroyed. And what we have apparently destroyed is apparently re-created.

Moving from our original and timeless nature into consciousness identified, we have created this circumstance in order to rediscover that the dream we are living has absolutely no purpose other than our awakening from it. That awakening emerges outside of the dream, outside of time, and is completely beyond the grasp of individual effort, path, process or belief.

Context

When very young I had a sense of being in a magic world, outside of time and the need to have to become or do anything... an unrecognised oneness that enveloped me simply in the wonder of what is. I feel it is the same for most children.

One day all of that changed and I entered the world of separation and need. I found that I had a separate mother and father, a name, and an apparent choice to do this or that. I moved into the world of time and space, boundary and exploration, endeavour, manipulation, and the pursuit of pleasure and avoidance of pain.

I came to own these experiences and believed they were my natural way of being.

I was also taught and came to believe that if I worked hard, behaved myself and succeeded in my chosen or imposed job, got married, had children and looked after my health, I stood a good chance of being happy. I did all of this quite successfully, and enjoyed myself at times, but I also recognised that something intangible and fundamental seemed to be missing. A secret of some kind.

Consequently I decided to seek out what was missing through religion.

Again I was told that if I worked hard and applied

myself to various disciplines, rituals and purifications, I would eventually come to deserve "spiritual fulfilment". Again I completely involved myself in whatever seemed appropriate, but still could not discover the reason for my sense of bereavement.

One day, almost as if by accident, I rediscovered the secret, or perhaps it rediscovered me.

To explain what happened is quite impossible. The description that comes nearest to it is that of being overwhelmed with a love and a total comprehension that is absolutely beyond imagination.

The revelation that accompanied this rediscovery was so simple and yet so revolutionary, that it swept away in a stroke all that I had been taught or had come to believe.

Part of that realisation was that enlightenment is absolutely beyond my effort to change the way I live, or even of changing life at all. It has to do with a total shift in the realisation of what it is that lives.

For I am already that which I seek. Whatever I seek or think I want, however long the shopping list may be, all of my desires are only a reflection of my longing to come home. And home is oneness, home is my original nature. It is right here, simply in what is. There is nowhere else I have to go, and nothing else I have to become.

Since that time I have embraced and lived that revelation - and avoided and rejected it.

It is of course impossible to communicate in words the inexpressible, and so this declaration is my attempt to express my understanding of that revelation. I try to explain the way in which my beliefs about enlightenment, time, purpose and my effort to achieve spiritual fulfilment, can directly interrupt that oneness that is continuously and directly available. How the illusion of separation, fear, guilt and abstraction can distract me from the freedom that includes and transforms these influences.

I also express in the best way I can how effortless and natural it is to let go and be open to that freedom.

To see this work as an exhortation to lead a meditative life or to "be here now", would be to entirely miss the point.

This declaration speaks about a singular and revolutionary leap in perception about what we really are. It requires no embellishment or lengthy explanation and once realised leaves nothing more to be said.

For the sake of clarity, the terms *enlightenment, liberation, fulfilment, freedom, oneness,* and so on, are all seen here as being the same as the absolute realisation by anyone of what they really are.

No Achievement

For me the first realisation of enlightenment, or of the nature of who I really am, is not something that can be expressed. What happened cannot even be called an experience, because the separate experiencer needed to be absent for it to emerge.

However, what accompanied that happening was a realisation of such simple magnitude and revolutionary content that it left me awestruck and quite alone.

One of the things I came to see is that enlightenment only becomes available when it has been accepted that it cannot be achieved.

Doctrines, processes and progressive paths which seek enlightenment only exacerbate the problem they address by reinforcing the idea that the self can find something that it presumes it has lost. It is that very effort, that investment in self-identity that continuously recreates the illusion of separation from oneness. This is the veil that we believe exists. It is the dream of individuality.

It is like someone who imagines that they are in a deep hole in the earth, and in order to escape they dig deeper and deeper, throwing the earth behind them and covering up the light that is already there.

The only likely effect of extreme effort to become that which I already am, is that eventually I will drop to the ground exhausted and let go.
In that letting go another possibility may arise.
But the temptation to avoid freedom through the sanctification of struggle is very attractive.
Struggle in time does not invite liberation.

Life is not a task. There is absolutely nothing to attain except the realisation that there is absolutely nothing to attain.

No amount of effort will ever persuade oneness to appear. All that is needed is a leap in perception, a different seeing, already inherent but unrecognised.

No-one Becomes Enlightened

I used to believe that people actually became enlightened, and that the event was similar to someone winning the jackpot in a national lottery. Once the prize had been won, the beneficiary would thereafter be guaranteed permanent bliss, infallibility and incorruptible goodness.

In my ignorance I thought these people had obtained and owned something that made them special and totally different from me. This illusory idea reinforced in me the belief that enlightenment was virtually unobtainable except for an extra-ordinary and chosen few. These misconceptions sprang from some image I held of how a state of perfection should look. I was not yet able to see that enlightenment has nothing to do with the idea of perfection. These beliefs were greatly strengthened when I compared my imagined inadequacies with the picture I held of whichever "spiritual hero" I happened to be attracted to at the time.

I feel that most people see enlightenment in a similar way.

Certainly there have been, and still are, many who seek to encourage such beliefs and who have actually claimed to have become enlightened.

I now see that this is as pointless a declaration as someone proclaiming to the world that they can breathe.

Essentially the realisation of enlightenment brings with it the sudden comprehension that there is no-one and nothing to be enlightened. Enlightenment simply is. It cannot be owned, just as it cannot be achieved or won like some trophy. All and everything is oneness, and all that we do is get in its way by trying to find it.

Those who make claims of enlightenment or take certain stances, have simply not realised its paradoxical nature and presume ownership of a state they imagine they have achieved. They are likely to have had a deep personal experience of some kind, but this bears absolutely no relationship to illumination. As a consequence they still remain locked into their own individualistic concepts based on their own particular belief systems.

These people often need to take on the role of "spiritual teachers" or "enlightened masters" and inevitably attract those who need to be students or disciples. Their teaching, still rooted in dualism, inevitably promotes a schism between the "teacher" and those who choose to follow the teaching. As the following increases so does the exclusive role of the master need to be enhanced.

One of the usual symptoms, when such a role has been adopted, is a clamp-down of any admission or sign of "human weakness". Together

with this a distance is usually created between "master" and followers.

As the specialness of the "master" becomes more effective, and the demands of the followers become greater, so invariably do the teachings become more obscure and convoluted. As the obscurity of the teachings increases, so does the schism get wider and many of the followers often become more confused and submissive. The usual effect on those involved can be unquestioning adulation, disillusionment, or an awakening and moving on.

However, these kinds of influences have established and maintained an illusory sense of doubt and inadequacy in the collective unconscious about people's ability to realise and allow something that is as natural, simple and available as breathing.

Those who have fully comprehended and embraced enlightenment have absolutely nothing to sell. When they share their understanding, they have no need to embellish themselves, or what they share. Neither do they have any interest in being mothers, fathers or teachers.

Exclusivity breeds exclusion, but freedom is shared through friendship.

Time

In my apparent separation I came to accept, without question, the existence and effect of time. Together with my belief in time I was inevitably married to the concept and experience of a beginning, a middle and an end... a journey towards the realisation of a goal or conclusion.

This concept of journey applied at any level, be it doing well at school, creating a successful business, or realising enlightenment. It was all a path to becoming - a reaching out for a result in time.

This message was etched most powerfully into my psyche by what appeared to be the process of birth and death. Such a mighty message reflected and reinforced the seeming irrefutability of time's existence, passage and effect. As I experienced what had appeared to be the effect of time, so did I come to believe in it. As I believed in the existence of time, so did I also come to believe in the limitation of my own existence. As I came to accept that limitation, so did I also come to believe that I needed to make use of the period given. I had to do something, achieve something, become something worthwhile during the time that I imagined remained. As a consequence the idea of purpose was born, and together with it my expectation and investment in what that purpose might bring.

Expectation and Purpose

I became locked into the limitation of time and separation through the expectation I had about purpose. I have been in pursuit of a variety of goals and purposes in my life, including spiritual ones. Within the traditional religious ethic, I have come across a kaleidoscope of western and eastern doctrines and concepts which I believed at the time represented a rich tradition of authoritative wisdom.

As a consequence of what I saw as my spiritual lack, I decided I had to do something - belong to something, become something worthwhile. I had to find a model of reality which would satisfy my need to feel I was making some sort of progress towards some sort of goal.

I decided to try to become a Christian.

Considering the information I had at the time, it seemed that this approach was appropriate. I had my western background, my knowledge of biblical history and tradition, the apparently unimpeachable truths, processes and rituals presented to me... original sin, prayer, confession, forgiveness, communion and purification, and the written and spoken word.

I felt I was doing my best with what at the time I

understood and sanctified, and what I anticipated and expected would give meaning to my spiritual life. If I tried harder, tomorrow would be better than today, another place would be better than this place.

I came to believe in the message of inadequacy which leads through repentance to a given grace, through which I would eventually be seen to deserve transition from a lower to a higher level of existence.

I now had the wherewithal I thought I needed to realise the purpose I believed would fulfil me.

I could solicit with prayer and negotiate through performance, whilst "God the Father" sat four square in heaven and kept the accounts.

It seemed there was so much opportunity, so much knowledge, and so much time in which to give meaning to my life, for it to become something better - something worthy. And my purpose was married to my hope. For it was the hope of better things to come which inspired me to struggle and strive, resist and persist in order to strengthen my sense of direction. I could now make spiritual progress for myself, and help others to do the same.

Purpose, hope and belief gave me the energy and the will to succeed. Purpose, hope and belief... these revered and seemingly powerful values which are acknowledged by many as so worthwhile. But of course they also live in the shadow of

confusion, hopelessness and despair. At the time I had not reckoned on that side of things. Eventually and inevitably the swinging pendulum of endless encounters with expectation and disappointment, effort and inadequacy, apparent strength and weakness, all played their part in my awakening from this dream.

All of those communions and confessions, and all of those spiritual tasks seemed endless... that greedy, bottomless, spiritual shopping basket that I would have to fill with prayer, abstinence, humility, worship and good deeds, and if I ever got to the bottom of that one I would have to fill another, probably beginning with obedience and chastity.

I tried and I tried, but it all seemed so archaic and joyless in some way. The expectation that an already fearful and inadequate follower could, through the discipline of negation and worship, become anything other than a fearful and inadequate follower, seemed as futile as the idea of celibacy being a route to celebration and whole-ness. I felt as though I was trying to bake a cake without any juice.

It seems to me that any attempt to translate the inexpressible into the doctrinal must inevitably end up as a misrepresentation... a contradictory idea about perfection which transforms the originator's subtle and beautiful song of freedom into an interminable dogma of limitation. When the bird has flown, the essence of its song is often mislaid

and then all we are left with is an empty cage.

I like the story of God and the Devil watching man as he discovered something beautiful in a desert. *"Aha"* said God to the Devil, *"now that man has found truth you will have nothing to do"*. *"On the contrary"* replied the Devil, *"I am going to help him organise it"*.

Whenever or wherever there is organised religion, there also can most easily flourish a rich breeding ground for our worst fears, our darkest guilt, and our ugliest conflicts, person to person, nation to nation and faith to faith. Whether we hold a religious belief or not, these wounds can lie deep within us and invade every part of our experience.

It felt unnatural and limiting to support an ethic based on such a purgative "no" and carefully considered "yes" when I intuitively recognised that what I was looking for was absolutely beyond both. In these circumstances I moved on and investigated the world of contemporary therapy and spirituality.

These approaches to fulfilment seemed to me to be so much more intelligent and accepting than anything I had previously come across, the ideas so very open and liberating.

It was tremendously exciting to be offered the means whereby I could learn to uncover, heal and integrate those parts of my life which seemed to

interfere with my relationships with people, creativity, health and wealth, and most importantly of all, my own sense of self-worth.

If all of us could do this, what a wonderful world it could become. It appealed to me, especially in contrast to the idea of having to shape myself to a way of life based on someone else's conceptual model of how I should be.

There were so many interesting and new processes to choose from, and so many people to share with in what felt like a twentieth century spiritual adventure. It was fascinating to be involved in shocking and illuminating break-throughs, the rush of emotions, the fear and excitement of revealing my innermost secrets, of truly surrendering to my guru, of discovering why I was so fascinated by and so frightened of women. Sharing in other people's agonies and revelations, past life memories, present assaults and future hopes and dreads, all was a revelation and a confirmation.

It was all so exciting, and it was all about me!

I involved myself in the deepest and most illuminating meditations, consumed the most recent and significant books, and of course threw myself with much enthusiasm into the latest therapies. They burst out of the ground like new fruits, to be sucked and digested, or tasted and thrown away... this breathing method, that

affirmation, this integration, that special and significant energy... all had a fascination for me in those early days. If these activities were seen to be introspective or self-indulgent, then I had already recognised that, with one exception, all choice is generated from self-motivation.

The expression of feelings became sacrosanct together with the need to think positively, forgive my mother, heal my inner child, delve into my past, and so on. All of these things became vital and important processes to follow... rather like a modern-day Ten Commandments.

I spent a year doing an intensive residential course experiencing many key contemporary therapies mixed with eastern meditations.

After a while I settled on those therapies or methods I felt suited me and brought me most benefit.

I experienced considerable movement of previously held inhibitions, and came to recognise belief systems and patterns that had strongly influenced much of my early behaviour.

In much of the work done it appears that the strengthening and reinforcement of a sense of self-identity and self-worth is the primary aim. The theory seems to be that if I can embrace and assimilate these processes, then I can eventually emerge as a more alive, balanced and effective individual, with a clear idea about relationships

and my part in the whole. All of that structure would need to be built on a powerful set of belief systems developed from considerable discipline and effort. But belief resides within the shadow of doubt. It only functions effectively in direct proportion to the suppression of the doubt that it seeks to override.

I began to see again that I was trying to repair and put together a set of parts in the hope that they might eventually come together to make a whole. But this approach directly contradicted my understanding that enlightenment lay beyond my efforts and expectations concerning self-identity and self-worth.

For those who seek change as individuals within the wheel of life, the contemporary therapeutic world offers tremendous scope and a much deeper and more accepting approach than anything that has gone before.

In my case the first realisation of enlightenment directly followed my moving on from the religious path when I was about twenty one years old. Some few years after this I involved myself in the contemporary therapies, thinking that they could be a vehicle for communicating the deeper possibility.

I have experienced that the kind of energy generated in certain therapeutic settings can open people to a deeper perception about the nature of

awareness and its implications.

But here again I had found myself occupied and fascinated by my expectations surrounding time, purposes and goals.

In the world of time, purposes and goals are perfectly appropriate, but there is so much investment placed on the attachment and expectations that surround them... becoming this, belonging to that, processes to change, or to be better, methods to purify, and so on. Important new people and places, masters of consciousness and teachers of truths spring up from everywhere and offer their own particular formula for living. And as we move from one to another we seem unwilling to see that freedom does not reside in one place or another simply because freedom, by its very nature, cannot be excluded or exclusive. We seem not to see that, as we march towards the next anticipated "spiritual" high, the treasure that we seek is to be discovered not in where we are going, but within the simple nature of the very footsteps that we take. In our rush to find a better situation in time, we trample over the flower of beingness that presents itself in every moment.

It seems to me that our attachment to purpose is born from our need to prove something to ourselves. But life is simply life, and is not trying to prove anything at all. This springtime will not try to be better than last springtime, and neither will an ash tree try to become an oak.

By letting go our fascination with the extra-ordinary and spectacular, we can allow ourselves to recognise the simple wonder that lies within the ordinary.

For life is its own purpose and doesn't need a reason to be. That is its beauty.

The Park

One day I was walking across a park in a suburb of London. I noticed as I walked that my mind was totally occupied with expectations about future events that might or might not happen. I seemed to choose to let go of these projections and simply be with my walking. I noticed that each footstep was totally unique in feel and pressure, and that it was there one moment and gone the next, never to be repeated in the same way ever again.

As all of this was happening there was a transition from me watching my walking to simply the presence of walking. What happened then is simply beyond description. I can only inadequately say in words that total stillness and presence seemed to descend over everything. All and everything became timeless and I no longer existed. I vanished and there was no longer an experiencer.

Oneness with all and everything was what happened. I can't say I was at one because I had disappeared. I can only say that oneness with all and everything was what happened, and an overwhelming love filled every part. Together with this there came a total comprehension of the whole. All of this happened in a timeless flash which seemed eternal.

Contained within and directly following this happening occurred a revelation so magnificent and revolutionary in its nature that I had to sit down on the grass in order to take in its consequence. What I saw was simple and obvious in one way but completely untranslatable in another. It was as if I had been given an answer that had no question. I had been shown a secret that is an open secret; and that all and everything that is known or unknown contains and reflects this open secret. Nature, people, birth and death, and our struggles, our fears and our desires are all contained within and reflect unconditional love.

I felt I had been suddenly overtaken and everything took on a new sense. I looked at grass, trees, dogs and people, moving as before, but now I not only recognised their essence but I was their essence, as they were mine. It was in another way as if everything, including me, was enveloped in a deep and all-encompassing love, and in a strange way it seemed that what I saw was also somehow nothing special... it is the norm that is not usually perceived.

Why me and why now? How could I have deserved to receive such a gift for nothing in return? I was certainly not pure in the biblical sense, or in any other recognised sense, or so my mind told me. I had not lived a disciplined life of meditation or of spiritual dedication of any kind. This illumination had occurred without any effort

on my part! I had apparently chosen to watch my walking in a very easy and natural way, and then this treasure had emerged.

I also came to recognise that this apparent gift had always been available and always would be. That was the most wonderful realisation of all! That utterly regardless of where, when or how I was, this presence was ready to emerge and embrace me. And this treasure was to be re-discovered not through arduous and seemingly significant spiritual practices and rituals. Not at all. This wonderful all-encompassing treasure was available within the essence of a footstep, in the sound of a tractor, in my feeling of boredom, in the sitting of a cat, in feelings of pain and rejection, on a mountaintop, or in the middle of Balham High Street. Anywhere and everywhere I am totally surrounded and embraced in stillness, unconditional love and oneness.

Later on I began to wonder how this treasure could be retained. But I have again and again come to see that what I had sought to rediscover can never be achieved or contained. There is nothing I have to do, and the very belief that I have to do anything to deserve this treasure, interrupts its inherent quality.

And this is again the paradox, for the divine instinct is continuously available, simply through the allowing of it. It is always at hand, in an eternal state of readiness... like the constant and faithful

lover it is ready to respond to our every call.

When I allow it, it is, when I avoid it, it is.

It requires no effort, demands no standards and holds no preferences.

Being timeless it sees no path to tread, no debt to pay. Because it acknowledges no right or wrong, neither does it recognise judgement or guilt. Its love is absolutely unconditional. It simply watches with clarity, compassion and delight as I move out for my return.

It is my birthright. It is my home. It is already that which I am.

Presence

If, however inadequately, enlightenment could be described in terms of qualities, I see them as unconditional love, compassion, stillness, and joy without cause. Existence in time is only a reflection of those qualities, and whilst I maintain and invest my belief in my separate identity, I can only again express a reflection of those qualities and not be their essence.

Whilst I do not know what I am, I am bereft.

Enlightenment, however, has another quality, which is the bridge between the timeless and my illusory sense of separation. That quality is presence. Presence is our constant nature but most of the time we are interrupting it by living in a state of expectation, motivation or interpretation. We are hardly ever at home. In order to rediscover our freedom we need to let go of these projections and allow the possibility of presence. Its real discovery, or our access to it, can only be made within the essence of what is. This is where spontaneous aliveness resides and where we can openly welcome the unknown.

Only here, in present awareness of simply what is, can there be freedom from self-image.

To live passionately is to let go of everything for

the wonder of timeless presence. When this apparently happens, there is a residing in the source of nothing and everything.

Presence is not to be confused with "being here now" which is a continuous process of the separate self and has no direct relevance to liberation.

Presence is a quality of welcoming, open awareness which is dedicated to simply what is. There can still be someone who is aware and there is that of which they are conscious... the sound of running water, the taste of tea, the feeling of fear, or the weight and texture of sitting on a seat. And then there can be a letting go of the one who is aware, and all that remains is presence. All of this is totally without judgement, analysis, wish to reach conclusion or to become. There is no traffic and no expectation. There is simply what is.

At first it is enough to allow dedicated aware-ness to what is. Letting go of the one who is aware can easily follow, but it can never be a task.

I cannot 'do' presence, simply because I am presence. So there is no process to learn because I cannot learn or achieve something that I already am.

Presence is totally effortless and is nearer to me than breathing. Presence can only be allowed and recognised. What I tend to do most of the time is sidestep it or interrupt it.

Existence would not be if it were not for presence. I am presence and you are presence. If we were not present, existence would not be.

Presence emanates from the source of all and everything known or unknown. And that is what we are. We are the sole source of our own unique manifestation.

There can be presence or we can remain separate. There can be openness or we can invest in manipulation. There can be a welcoming of the continuous simplicity and wonder of simply what is or we can be imprisoned by the limitations of our expectations. All is appropriate.

Presence is the light in the darkness. It is atomic. One moment of presence brings more light to the world than a thousand years of "good works". In presence all action is uncluttered and unsullied. It is spontaneity born from stillness.

In allowing presence, however, we embrace a kind of death. What dies is all expectation, judgement and effort to become. What dies is the stuff of separation, the sense of self-identity, which can only function in the illusory world of past and future, memory and expectation. For it will be found that if we let go into simply what is, we will be in a place of unknowing.

That is how the embracing of presence is a kind of death. What dies is the dream of individuality. What we let go of is our incessant need to feel that

we are a separate entity... that we will continue as a fraction of the whole. And in that letting go we come to see that all death is a rebirth into liberation.

For what we open up to in presence is the possibility of entering oneness, the rediscovery of what we really are. This is the bridge between the world of separation and enlightenment which once crossed, is no more.

When there is presence the self is no more. We stand astride the living paradox and allow the emergence of freedom from the incessant traffic of becoming. It is a welcoming of the open secret.

When there is presence there is awareness and this is the light that enters the darkness. The light enters the darkness and dissipates those illusions that appear to interrupt oneness. Awareness does not divide or suppress and thereby give energy to the unreal. It simply sees what is and brings the light which allows that which is illusory to evaporate.

There is never any situation in which we cannot be united with the present. Isn't that wonderful?! I will say it again. Presence is available in any situation, or put another way, freedom is already continuously available.

There is sufficient in every day to be present with... pain, fear, the sound of a car, wind in the trees, my body in the chair, a pen in my fingers, emotional pain, habits, abounding self-judgement, guilt, walking, the taste of cheese, being in a hurry, being lazy, being in control, and the guru mind which insists that presence is non-productive and that I should be doing something "spiritual", or at the very least, useful. Presence shines wherever it will, on any part of existence.

If I try to bring light to one aspect of my story in particular, I disturb the natural flow and counter-point of the opportunities that life and my innate wisdom presents to me. For presence is not a task, and it cannot be used by my will. It is not a spiritual exercise or a tool to get somewhere, like prayer or formal meditation. Directly I attempt to harness it to a task I have already tried to constrain that which is beyond limitation.

Presence is all-encompassing and is its own reward. It isn't trying to get anywhere, and if I am, I have already interrupted it.

However, when there is presence the whole being relaxes into its embrace. There are no more questions and there is no more striving. The mind departs the throne, the body relaxes, the breathing evens out and the perception becomes global. I rest in that which never comes and never goes away.

When there is presence there is total intimacy and the senses are heightened to a degree previously unrecognised... I see and touch in innocence, I taste and smell for the first time, and hear a new sound that is vital, fresh and unknown.

There is a subtle feeling of risk and serenity in presence. It is the first and last step. It moves beyond time and self-identity and provides the ground in which the discovery of what I am is made immediately and directly available.

When there is presence, all that is illusory falls away, and what is left is real, vital and passionately alive. Life full on... not my life, not anyone's life, but simply life.

Presence does not bring heaven down to earth or raise earth up to heaven. All is one.

The Choiceless Choice

In presence I see that I have never chosen or done anything, but have only been lived through.

And so I have never stopped the sea or moved the sun or taken one step nearer or further away from my birthright.

In accepting my divine helplessness I enjoy the freedom of never having a past or future I could call my own.

Some people ask, "Who chooses, who directs this wonderful chaos?" But once in the arms of the beloved nothing matters, and I can live as though I choose and rejoice in the letting go.

My World

In what I experience as my world everything is totally unique for me. No-one else can know my experience of the colour red, my taste of tea, my feelings of fear and happiness, of walking, of dreaming, or of waking.

In time my experiences largely shape my beliefs, and what I believe I again come to experience. It is the interplay of these two compatriots that seem to influence my life story, moment by moment, day by day, and so on.

At this level of existence I appear to be the producer, script-writer, director of cast, script and music, in a film called "My Story".

When I look back at my life as openly as possible, I see how I have attracted to me the people, the events and the patterns that have been perfectly appropriate to the kinds of influences and images that my particular belief systems have been broadcasting.

Many people have become very excited about this concept and have suggested and taught that if we can change our thought patterns and our belief systems, then we can change the way we experience life. It seems this could be so, but they also entirely miss the point. For what we really are is

beyond the limitation of experience and belief.

Until I have rediscovered what I am, what kind of existence am I trying to create? From where do I see clearly that what I think I want is what I really need? Will my idea of what I should create be better than yours, or will our individual visions clash? That appears to be the recurring pattern.

What is possibly not realised by those who would pursue this concept is that beyond all of our wishes and desires to create what we think we want, there is a hidden agenda... another and much more powerful principle of unconditional love that is continuously functioning, entirely inherent but usually unrecognised. It is the very core of the living paradox.

All of existence as we know it, within the limitations of time, is only a reflection of that hidden principle which is continuously inviting us to remember what we really are. Within that reflection there is no right or wrong, better or worse, but only the invitation.

For whilst we remain locked within the experience of being separate individuals having to negotiate with existence, we remain in a state of dreaming.

In that dream state, all that we do is governed by the law of opposites in which all that is seen as positive is exactly and equally balanced by its

opposite. Through deep reflection we come to discover that we are on a wheel in which everything repeats itself over and over again in differing images. What we apparently create we destroy and what we apparently destroy we re-create again.

And despite what we might believe about free will and choice, we come to see that we are dreamed characters in a divine play reacting and responding from a set of conditioned reflexes and belief systems. All of our dream world that we see as progressive comes within the parameters of this perfectly balanced and exactly neutral state which serves only to reflect another possibility.

We are the dreamers in this dream which has absolutely no purpose other than our awakening from it.

In reality we are surrounded by and embraced in unconditional love, whether we respond to it or not. Our experience in time sets up a perfectly appropriate manifestation, exactly suited in its grand happenings and tiny nuances, to the particular and unique needs of our re-awakening. The source of the hidden principle is ourselves, and it is fired by our longing to come home.

And however significant or insignificant we think our activities are, however talented, artistic, useful, ordinary or fruitless we may feel our

expression in the world appears to be, all of this is simply and only a function of that hidden principle. A totally appropriate reflection providing the never-ending opportunity to enter into and beyond all phenomena and rediscover the source of its emanation.

The Death of the Mind/Body

The death of the mind/body is only the ending of the illusion of a journey in time.

The awakening to unconditional love is immediate. We are enveloped in our original nature regardless of anything that apparently happened.

When the body/mind is dropped there is no intermediary process of preparation or purification. How can there be? Who was there? All ideas of a personal "after life" or re-incarnation are merely the mind wishing to preserve the illusion of its continuity.

The story is over. The divine novel has been written and, regardless of how the mind might judge, not one jot could have been different.

The scenery evaporates and the characters have left the stage... their apparent existence begins and ends with the dream that has been played out.

And yet, nothing has happened. For we are already the ocean, the waves, the darkness and the light, the nothing and the everything.

Abstraction

I have been fascinated and waylaid by abstraction, painting the picture I would rather have in preference to living the experience I would rather not have.

What I abstract never comes to be, or only sometimes flickers into life like a watered-down approximation.

My abstraction is a smoke-screen born from longing or frustration, and it offers me a holiday of dreams. It is always safe, predictable, and an indulgence in the known.

If I drop abstraction and move my awareness, for instance, to my bodily sensations, I discover there is a symphony going on. Not necessarily in tune, but nevertheless constantly changing and moving, coming and going. Something is happening here or there... it evaporates and something else takes its place. There is very little that I can control or manipulate. It is immeasurable and unknown, being and then not being.

In the same way, if I let go and listen, touch, taste, smell, or see, there is no way of knowing beforehand the exact quality of those sensations. I could say that I can anticipate the sound of a bird singing, but it is only information based on memory.

It is not alive, vital and unknown. The sound I actually hear, the sound of what is, will not be the same as my abstraction of it. When I first listen to the sound I will try to grasp it and label it in order to control it. When I let go of that control, there is simply the listener and the sound. When the listener is dropped, there is only the sound.
I am no longer there - there is simply the naked and vibrant energy of what is. Nothing is needed, all is fulfilled.

It is within the very alchemy of this timeless presence that freedom resides.

Life beckons me. It whispers, it calls me and in the end it screams at me. The scream of crisis or disease is often what will bring me to the rediscovery of who I really am, for it is difficult to abstract suffering.

Fear

Until I recognise who I really am, my life can be largely driven by that which I fear.

It can be my fear that engenders my belief in a beginning and an end.

It is my fear of losing myself that can perpetuate and sustain my drive to survive and continue, and what I long for and fear most is the absence of my self.

Fearing weakness I strive for control, fearing intimacy I strive to be aloof, fearing subservience I strive to be dominant, and if I fear being ordinary I try to be special.

The things I can be afraid of are endless, because if one fear is overcome I can put another one in its place.

If there is present awareness, fear is seen clearly as an abstraction... a future anxiety born from memory's blueprint. If the story that engenders the fear is dropped, I discover that all I am left with is a physical sensation which is raw and alive. Now it ceases to overrun me and quietly takes its place in existence. It is the same with physical or emotional pain. When I cease to own it I liberate myself from its bondage and see it simply as it is.

If I cease to label suffering as bad, and mine, it is possible to allow it simply as energy in a certain form, and it can then begin to have its own flavour which can take me deeply into presence.

The nature of suffering is that it speaks deeply to me of another possibility. By desiring pleasure and avoiding pain I chop in two the very root of that possibility.

Guilt

I can only feel guilty if I judge who I am from a set of belief systems that I have been taught or that I have constructed for myself. My self-constructed beliefs again can only emanate from my past experiences in time. These concepts are linked to the idea of a journey towards a goal, a path to purification.

In presence there is no becoming, no attachment to a goal. I see that I no longer have to achieve any standard or behave in a certain way in order to become worthy.

Whilst I expend my energy in feeling guilty and attempting to assuage that illusory sense, I continuously negate the possibility of liberation. There is a fascination and an indulgence built into the drama of sin, or karma, which can powerfully smoke-screen the very real avoidance of the rediscovery of what I am. What I am doing is investing in an illusory concept about right or wrong in order to avoid that which is absolutely beyond both.

In presence there is no debt because there is no history. In any situation either I feel separate or there is presence. In separation, no matter what happens I feel separate. In presence, the self is no more and there is simply that which is.

Either situation is complete. Each happening is its own reward. It is there and then it is gone. There is no further ongoing debt to pay.

Whilst we continuously employ the remorseless judge to calculate and measure everything we do or are, we imprison ourselves in an existence of struggle, guilt and suffering, only to appease a god that is ourselves projected.

There is only the knowing or the unknowing. If I cannot understand, I cannot see, and darkness is simply darkness. It is neither right nor wrong.

All concepts of bad or good, original sin, karma or debt of any kind, are the products of an unawakened mind that is locked into time and the maintenance and reinforcement of a sense of father, mother and self.

Thinking

My thinking creates time and time creates my thinking. Within time thinking I maintain my illusory sense of self-identity and separation... I think, therefore I continue.

My thinking in time, in the main, grasps and divides, continuously producing ideas of progress towards satisfaction or calamity. It disturbs and speaks of order and makes promises and speaks of destruction.

My time thinking moves backward and forward over a sea of memories and projections from a place I call myself.

My mind maintains the immaculate balance between limitation and liberation at the same time looking for lifetimes in every part of existence, in the seen and unseen, searching and longing, to discover only the one that is looking.

No amount of thinking will tell me what I am, but understanding can take me to the river's edge.

Stillness is not brought about by not thinking. Stillness is absolutely beyond the presence or absence of thought. I cannot make myself still, but when that which appears not to be still is seen, then that seeing emanates from stillness.

Creative thinking emerges from stillness.

But if I move beyond thinking, where am I and who am I?

Relationships

My early experiences with parents and others sets up my beliefs and my patterns about relationships, and these patterns follow and influence every relationship thereafter until I rediscover who I am.

In whatever game I play, those to whom I relate will, in the main, become compatriots in that game and reinforce and support it. If I need to be needed I will create the needy. If I need to be rejected then I will attract rejection. There are as many variations as there are people. But patterns are only a confirmation of my particular needs and beliefs, and they reflect that which I have not yet rediscovered. They are perfectly appropriate - simply a part of the hidden principle of unconditional love inviting me to see another possibility.

What I experience as a relationship in my world of time and separation, seems like a link between me and another. It can be an exchange of feelings, interests and enthusiasms, laughter and tears, thoughts and reflections. One part communicating with another part. I am relating to that which I project out there, apart from me. There is very little merging in the fullest sense. It seems like a communication between two projections, two conditionings, two patterns, or an agreement to stroke each other's egos.

When I first meet somebody my computer sometimes places the other person in a box in which I keep them imprisoned. Sometimes I will extend bits of the box here and there, or I will make it bigger or smaller. In this way I stay safe and relate to my concepts about the person rather than who they really are.

When I strive to become that which I think is my cause, I can live in a state of comparison with others or see them as my judge. It is a kind of subtle competition.

I can also see the other person as someone who I believe can fulfil my sense of lack. They can acknowledge the image that I wish to project, or they can reinforce my sense of being worthy. They can excite me and comfort me with their presence. They fulfil a need.

The way in which I relate to others is a most powerful reflection in the most fundamental relationship of all, and that is with myself.

When I have rediscovered who I am, however, there is no longer any question of relationships. In this open and welcoming presence there is no need for memory or repetition, comparison or expectation. No place for one part meeting another. There is no distance between the two and therefore nothing needs to relate.

All of our energy is merged into a continual freshness, and the celebration of simply what is.

It is a communion of spontaneous giving and receiving that can enlighten those times when we return to relating. Often there is silence because there is no need to fill the void once seen as threatening. These silences are full of simply being together in an existence that is continually dancing.

I am not . . .

. . . my life story, the mind, the body, feelings, experiences of pain or pleasure, struggle, success or failure. I am not loneliness, stillness, frustration or compassion. I am not even what I think is my purpose, the seeking, the finding, or anything which is called a spiritual experience.

When I don't know what I am I sanctify these experiences, take ownership of them and give them great significance. I believe they mean something which, once understood, will give me answers and provide formulas. But these experiences are only consciousness concealing and revealing itself in order to be recognised. When I know what I am I discover that I am not existence, I am the presence which allows existence to be. Existence either blossoms in that presence or reflects back my sense of separation.

I am . . .

. . . the divine expression exactly as I am, right here, right now. You are the divine expression exactly as you are, right here, right now. It is the divine expression, exactly as it is, right here, right now. Nothing, absolutely nothing, needs to be added or taken away. Nothing is more valid or sacred than anything else. No conditions need to be fulfilled. The infinite is not somewhere else waiting for us to become worthy.

I do not have to experience 'the dark night of the soul', or surrender, be purified, or go through any kind of change or process. How can the illusory separate self practise something in order to reveal that it is illusory?

I don't need to be serious, honest, dishonest, moral or immoral, aesthetic or gross. There are no reference points. The life story that has apparently happened is uniquely and exactly appropriate for each awakening. All is just as it should be, right now. Not because it is a potential for something better, but simply because all that is, is divine expression.

The invitation to discover that there is no-one who needs liberating is constant. There is no need to wait for moments of transformation, to look for

the non-doer, permanent bliss, an ego-less state, or a still mind.

I don't even have to wait for grace to descend. For I am, you are, it is already the abiding grace.

Seen and Unseen

This is a book declaring that enlightenment is a sudden, direct and energetic illumination that is continuously available. It is the open secret which reveals itself in every part of our lives. No effort, path of purification, process or teaching of any kind can take us there. For the open secret is not about our effort to change the way we live. It is about the rediscovery of what it is that lives.

No one concept, or set of concepts, can express enlightenment. To attempt to share through words the rediscovery and wonder of what we are is as futile a process as writing a recipe for plum pudding and expecting someone reading it to be able to taste it.

It seems to me that verbal communication can only ever be an expression of an understanding, and I am sharing my understanding of what I feel is the most significant and liberating insight that it is possible to comprehend.

There is nothing new that is being expressed here. We all have a sense of it, and it has been written and spoken about in various ways and from differing influences and backgrounds.

Some people I have shared this with have put it away in a box with a label on it. Many have come

across it and quickly shuffled back to that which they think they can know and do. Others have said that "life is not that simple". I have to say that simplicity was one of the most wonderful qualities that surprised me about this revelation, together with its all-encompassing nature. There are those who believe that "enlightenment takes time" or that they need to experience various processes or realise certain beliefs before considering "this kind of approach". Some have complained that they have used present awareness and "nothing has changed or got better"?! Others vigorously reject the idea that freedom can be realised in any other way than through effort, sacrifice and discipline. And some have heard, and made the leap in their own unique way.

But from wherever and whenever this insight is communicated, it has no connection with end-gaining, belief, path or process. It cannot be taught but is continuously shared. Because it is our inheritance, no-one can lay claim to it. It needs not to be argued, proven or embellished, for it stands alone simply as it is, and can only remain unrecognised and rejected, or realised and lived.

Tony Parsons, 1995

Tony Parsons leads meetings, discussions and residentials in the UK and internationally.

For details, visit the website at:
http://www.theopensecret.com

alternatively

You can write to Tony Parsons at:
Tony Parsons
P. O. Box 117
Shaftesbury
SP7 9WB